The 'Nature' of West Dunbartonshire

Four Summer Walks

by

Paul Murdoch

Most photographs were taken by Paul Murdoch
Additional shots *Harvey Smart

Visit Paul Murdoch on The Scottish Book Trust website

Details of author visits and much more at
www.paulmurdoch.co.uk

'Paul Murdoch - photographer, writer and narrator for the Clydesider, takes a look at some of the wildlife and history of West Dunbartonshire through a series of four summer walks. His pictures and descriptions make this volume a beautiful snapshot of the area...' - Gordon Wallace

INTRODUCTION

Having lived in West Dunbartonshire all my life, it was difficult to know where to begin. What walk could I take you on first? What birds and insects would we find? Who trod these paths before us and why? What legacies did they leave? How has our home and the nature within it changed over the years?

Within striking distance of Loch Lomond and the Kirkpatrick Hills there is a massive variety of landscapes and ecologies in West Dunbartonshire. With the natural flow of fresh water from the River Leven onto the Clyde Estuary, the biodiversity is still rich here. Nature has claimed back much of the industrial past. The toppled mills, chimneys and workshops are now covered in a thick layer of new life that invades and permeates the valley floor. While many of our docks and shipyards have been redeveloped, green space is usually in abundance and already a haven for new life.

Above us, on the moors and cliffs, time has stood still to a degree. The ebb and flow of migratory birds like the cuckoo and the meadow pipit may be out of kilter a little but remains largely unchanged.

The lichens and mosses that cover our ancient forts still cling onto the past while the heather and ferns that carpet our hills stretch up from forests still teeming with life.

Meadow Pipit

Much of what you will see in this book is hidden nature. Things we never notice in everyday life because we're too busy living that life. We might hear a cuckoo call in the distance or the occasional screech of a buzzard above our heads but it's doubtful that we'll actually pause long enough to take in the full extent of what actually goes on around us every second of every day.

Look in any direction and there are probably a million tiny heartbeats within a few steps - in the air, under our feet or just out of sight.

This book is about stopping. It's about turning off the phone. Come on! Just for a few minutes... It's about finding a spot with a view and sitting down. It's about getting things in perspective.

I've always thought of myself as 'a dot on a dot'. We are, at this very moment, lucky enough to be alive on the

Ringlet Butterfly

third rock from a sun on a world that teems with life, despite everything we are doing to its detriment. We're on a so-called *Goldilocks Planet* that has just the right amount of stuff it needs to support life.

Zooming out from, let's say, the first place I'm going to take you - Pappert Well, there are an estimated 300 million other Goldilocks planets in our galaxy alone. And get this... There are around 200 billion galaxies in our Universe.

People have asked me why I'm using the word 'nature' in the title when I also talk about our buildings and monuments. Well, we might regard ourselves as very special, and we are, but we are also just one of the many species here. We even have a name - *Homo sapiens*.

If an alien ever makes it here from one of those far off planets and has a David Attenborough equivalent, he

Common Wasp

might compare us to wasps. You get solitary wasps but many also live in huge colonies, in structures they have built using stuff they have gathered or even manufactured. Nests are part of nature.

Then he'd see us and realise that we've done the same. We've also built structures from stuff all around us.

That's why I regard buildings like the Torpedo Factory in Alexandria or Clydebank Town Hall as nature.

However, that Attenborough alien might then look at the fossil record and see that wasps have been successful for 240 million years, whereas the humans have only been here for 2 million. He may also deduce that the wasps have been, and continue to be, better for the planet.

I wonder where he'd spray the pesticide?

I realise that perspective is relative, but it might be worth slowing down a little. Something most of us were forced to do during Covid.

Personally, I was forced to take the time to look closer again. Regain some of my childhood 'sense of wonder'.

As the pace of life quickens again, it gets more and more difficult to remember, to pause and breathe it all in. But I try…

So, back to my mission - to take you on four mindful summer walks in West Dunbartonshire.

There is no need to do any of these walks in their entirety. It's fine to dip in and out of different sections. Do 1km one weekend and another bit later. Walking should be a pleasurable journey where you learn and appreciate things. Not an endurance test.

I've highlighted any actual directions in blue… but always refer to the map at the beginning of each chapter if stuck.

Videos of the walks should come on stream in 2023. Updates will be posted on - www.paulmurdoch.co.uk/nature

But remember - 'Getting lost is never a waste of time…'

It's always a good idea to take some water and fruit. Even a phone, if absolutely necessary.

Oh, I should explain - the reason I'm doing these books in four seasons is because the nature you will find 'out there' is very different during each period. The birds, the animals, the flowers, the insects…the whole vibe varies.

Acknowledgements

I would like to thank Mary Irvine and John O'Hare for their support during the writing of this book. Also The Vale Of Leven History Facebook Group for the wonderful information in their posts which inspired me to delve into the history of the area.

Walk One

Renton Station - Pappert Well

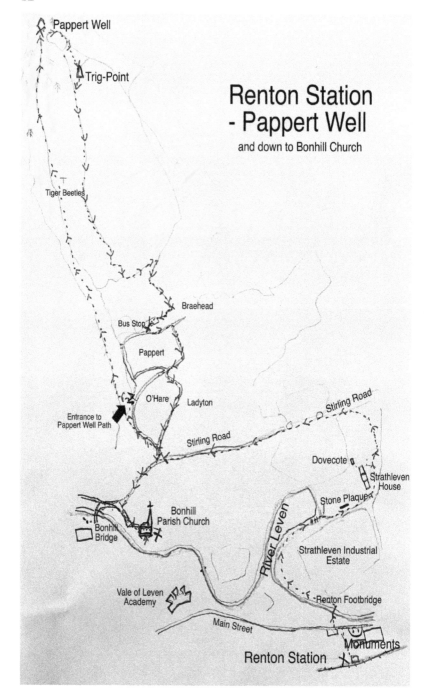

Renton Station - Pappert Well

and down to Bonhill Church

Pappert Well

Trig-Point

Tiger Beetles

Braehead

Bus Stop

Pappert

O'Hare   Ladyton

Entrance to
Pappert Well Path

Stirling Road

Stirling Road

Dovecote

Strathleven
House

Stone Plaque

Bonhill
Parish Church

Bonhill
Bridge

River Leven

Strathleven Industrial
Estate

Vale of Leven
Academy

Renton Footbridge

Main Street

Monuments

Renton Station

8km Medium **- quite steep and muddy in places**

<u>The start of the walk</u>

Renton Railway Station - Strathleven House

Opened in July 1850, the station used to have double tracks until 1986, when it was reduced to single track. The station building was taken over by the Strathleven Artizans in 2010 during Scotrail's 'adopt a station' initiative.

If open, it's worth taking a look here at their collection of items associated with the Outlaw King - Robert the Bruce, who was said to have lived in Strathleven Park. They have a throne said to be carved from a great oak tree that unfortunately toppled after it was set on fire in

2004. The oak, known as the Bruce Tree, was thought to have been over 700 years old, which could tie in with the man himself. Bruce defeated the English at Bannockburn in 1314.

Leaving Renton Station walk down towards the Main Street and turn right towards the new £15.1 million Renton School Campus. This is where you will find two very important monuments.

Erected in 1922, the smaller and squarer of the two, the 25ft war memorial, was originally located at the Howgate, opposite the football grounds in Renton. Now on Main Street, it commemorates the 158 men who died in WW1 and another 55 poor souls who perished in WW2. Shockingly, the original bronze plaques containing the names of the fallen were stolen in the 1980's. They've since been replaced with stone tablets.

Right beside it, the Smollett monument, erected in 1775 celebrates the life of Tobias Smollett. An important literary figure, he helped establish the novel as a writing construct. He was born nearby in Dalquhurn House. At 60ft high, his column is quite a landmark.

The Latin inscription, updated by Dr Samuel Johnson, describes how Tobias died at the age of 51 and praises his literary works. It also tells us that his body lies in a place called Leghorn in Italy.

Head back along Main Street until your reach The Central Bar.

The site of a watering hole since the 1700s, it's regarded by some as a Heritage pub. One of just 30 in Scotland, it's recognised for its authentic interior.

It's been used as a location in several film and TV productions, including the 2016 remake of 'Whisky Galore' and 'Young Adam', a 2003 film starring Ewan McGregor.

The River Leven runs a little slower here and you might spot a cormorant resting on the rocks.

Cormorant

One of our most iconic birds, the cormorant is surrounded by myths and legends. In the Greek story of Odysseus, a cormorant saves the hero after a great storm by giving him a 'life jacket'. In Norway cormorants flying together signify a message from the dead.

Even now, the bird is seen as a good luck talisman for fishermen. In China they actually train them to fish, tethering the bird by its throat so it can't swallow the catch.

Thankfully, here you're more likely to see a cormorant flying fast and low over the water. Or perhaps resting by the shore, like the one in the picture.

Their name comes from two Latin words, *corvus* and *marinus* meaning 'Raven of the sea'. Strangely, they share a slightly disgusting habit with owls. They regurgitate pellets made of the compressed bones and skin of their prey.

Common Frog

In the case of cormorants that can be fish, eels or even sea snakes.

I don't think you'll find many sea snakes in West Dumbartonshire, but you might find a frog on the grassy bank as you walk down to the footbridge.

The footbridge connects Renton to the Strathleven Industrial Estate which was developed in the 1950s. The 100m long structure allowed the local workforce easy access to companies like Polaroid, Westclox, Burroughs, Turnkey and many more businesses that eventually replaced the old textile industries.

Coming down the steep steps into Strathleven there are a good number of wild flowers to be found in summer.

Ground Elder and Hogweed line the path and it's on these white flower-heads that you'll find some interesting insects. I especially like the soldier beetle. Often found in little groups, they congregate to mate and feed.

Soldier Beetles

The soldier beetle gets its name from the colour of its elytra. That's the two hardened wings on its back that cover the functioning wings below. It reminded people of the uniform of an English soldier - hence the name. Omnivores, they eat pollen and nectar as well as aphids. They're attracted to yellows and whites, and prefer a flower that forms a platform. They have to pack lots in during their short three-month life, so mating and feeding are done at the same time. A quarter of all species on earth are beetles. We have about two and a half thousand different kinds in Scotland alone.

At the base of the footbridge, turn left along the trail that follows the river's meandering path back towards Alexandria and Bonhill.

It's on this section that you're quite likely to see a Grey Heron. Here, perched on a tree, the Heron can be quite a timid bird, often flying off if you get too close.

Grey Heron

With a wingspan of six feet it's one of our biggest birds. Now protected, it used to be on the menu in times gone by. Especially the younger birds which were called *branchers*.

Although this particular bird was preening to keep its feathers waterproof, you'll see them hunting fish, frogs and small mammals by the waterside. They raise their young in heronries, some containing up to four hundred individual nests at a time.

With the river on your left you will wind your way through woodland eventually reaching a set of rough steps that lead you up towards the edge of the industrial estate.

You will soon find a fork in the path. Take the right-hand fork and follow the path that edges the industrial

estate perimeter fence. Walking along the fence you will then come onto a road called Burroughs Way. About half-way along you'll find a small brick wall.

The almost indecipherable plaques tell of visits made to the Strathleven Industrial site by Queen Elizabeth 11.

Royal Plaques

The longer plaque celebrates her visit in April 1953 while the lower one commemorates her appearance in the June of 1971.

This pretty tired-looking plaque once stood close to the Westclox Factory which produced over 50 million clocks, and employed over a thousand locals at its peak.

Walk on from here towards the corner of the road. Looking up the hill, you'll find the very impressive Strathleven House.

Strathleven House

Strathleven House to the start of the Pappert Well track.

Built in 1700 by William Cochrane who, after the union in 1707, became an MP in London, it was originally named Levenside House. The Cochrane's coat of arms can still be seen on the front gable, next to the Graham coat of arms.

The Graham coat of arms references his wife - daughter of James Graham and 2nd Marquess of Montrose. As an aside, there is a legend that Gramus, a chief of Caledonia, tore down part of the Antonine Wall. This May have some bearing on the Graham coat of arms which normally depicts a stork.

Coats of Arms

Eventually falling into the hands of James Ewing in 1830, it was renamed Strathleven House. He made various alterations and additions such as a new stable block.

His widow lived there right up until 1900 when it was inherited by the Crum-Ewing family.

An interesting outbuilding is the dovecote, just to the side of the main house. It's said that a piece of the Antonine Wall, namely - a Roman distance stone, was once built into the structure. This was removed in 1942

Strathleven Dovecote

and apparently resides in The Glasgow Art Galleries and Museum.

In 1947 the estate was earmarked as a potential industrial estate and work soon began to transform the site.

The house fell into disrepair but was restored in 2000. It's now used by various companies as office space.

There is still substantial open space up from the house and a track will take you all the way up through meadows dotted with mature trees to the Stirling Road.

Again, it's worth keeping your eyes pealed here as this is an ideal spot for Roe Deer, Great Spotted Woodpeckers and Buzzards. The Great Spotted Woodpecker will often come into local gardens to feed on peanuts or fat balls.

Great Spotted Woodpecker

Heading along the Stirling road pavement go past two mini roundabouts and continue on until there is a right turn into the O'Hare Estate. Walk up the steep path that has the trees and bushes on your left, past some fenced off playgrounds, until you get to a sign that says 'Pappert Well - Community Woodland'. There's also a barrier that's supposed to stop motorbikes and quads.

Entrance to Pappert Well Track to Pappert Well

Now follow the track through the woods and over the stream until you're on a path that has woods and deep gullies to your right and fields on your left.

You are now on the track that will take you all the way up to the well.

As you continue into the woods and up the path you might see Chaffinches in the birch trees or on a stone dyke.

Entrance to Pappert Well Track

You'll eventually come to a style which you cross and edge around a small burn. In summer you might see Meadow Brown, Small Copper and Ringlet Butterflies here.

If you're really lucky you might spot a Golden-ringed Dragonfly.

They breed in boggy acidic rivers and the female is the UK's longest dragonfly at 8.4cm. If you get close enough to a basking female you'll see her amazing green eyes. With 360 degree vision they view the world in a mosaic of colour.

These mid-air hunters will snatch all sorts of other insects like butterflies, bumble bees, damsel flies, beetles and even wasps.

Golden-ringed Dragonfly

The larvae live, for up to five years, at the bottom of the streams and rivers where they ambush tiny fish, tadpoles and insects.

The males are very territorial and would break the speed limit in most towns, reaching an incredible 34mph.

As the path opens up a little, you get good views of the Vale of Leven and eventually reach a more moor-like terrain with conifers to either side.

It's here, as you walk up the path, that you may catch a glimpse of a Brown Hare or some Roe Deer.

Hares tend to be very shy and may have leverets in the summer that they need to keep hidden. Much bigger than rabbits with longer ears, they'll be on the look out for Buzzards, Ravens and Carrion Crows, all of which are more than capable of taking their young.

Brown Hare

However, don't forget to look down at the path your walking on. Apart from an army of wolf spiders carrying tiny spiderlings on their backs, you'll probably notice a flash of green.

A voracious predator of the mountain track, the Tiger Beetle has got to be one of our most colourful and dramatic creatures.

There are various varieties but the one you're most likely to see here, in the summer months, is the Green Tiger Beetle.

Fast fliers as well as rapid runners, they like sandy or chalky soils and enjoy basking in the sun. You can see, from the beetle picture, how sandy the soil becomes on this section of the hill. The white sensory hairs on its legs pick up vibrations and the formidable mouthparts will easily deal with those spiders mentioned earlier.

Green Tiger Beetle*

If you disturb them they'll probably fly for a short distance before scurrying into the grass and heather.

Keep climbing up the path until you reach the tree line. It can be muddy here and you may have to duck below branches and edge round some of the wetter areas, but eventually you'll see a clearing with a very obvious, low, horseshoe-shaped wall.

Pappert Well from above

Pappert Well to Braehead Bus Stop

Close to an old drover's road that came all the way from Falkirk, Pappert Well was a known stopping point where people and their animals could have a drink.

The Spring

The well is actually part of the local hydrosphere. A spring that comes all the way from a deep layer of water-bearing rock that forms part of the Earth's crust, you can actually see the water bubbling up through the particles of sand.

Once at the well, you can either retrace your steps and go back down the same track you came up, or you can head south through the trees that edge the clearing in the picture labelled 'The Spring'.

I'd do the latter. Soon you'll be on a much more open moor with a track leading to a trig-point (concrete, four-sided marker stone) on a small, heathery knoll.

Small Copper

Once you reach the trig-point, you'll get a fantastic view of the Clyde, the Vale of Leven and even Loch Lomond.

You might see a Small Copper Butterfly on your way back down from here.

You will certainly see lots of moorland plants on your descent.

The picture above shows - *Devil's Bit with a Cader Bumblebee in attendance, the Common Spotted Orchid, Bog Asphodel, the Heath Spotted Orchid and the Greater Butterfly Orchid.*

The Bog Asphodel starts off as a bright-yellow, spiky flower in early summer and turns a bright russet orange, as shown in the picture, in August. Its Latin name *ossifragum* literally means 'bone breaker'.

Found on peaty, damp ground, it was thought that animals grazing on it got brittle bones. However, it was actually the low calcium levels in the soil. It grows well on these soils, so any animals feeding nearby won't get the correct minerals needed to maintain their bone density.

The Whitethroat

Winding down through the trees towards the housing estates, you might spy a Whitethroat. I've seen this pretty bird just behind the fence that divides the hill from the houses in Braehead in the summer months.

From the hill, there's a cut through the Braehead fence. It's best, however, to turn a sharp right here and walk up into a little square and car-park, as shown, in the adjoining Pappert estate.

From here, you can exit the square and turn sharp right. You'll now find yourself at the bus stop.

The 206 will take you back down into Alexandria.

Braehead to Bonhill Parish Church

However, if you want to extend your walk a little and take in a few more sights…walk this way.

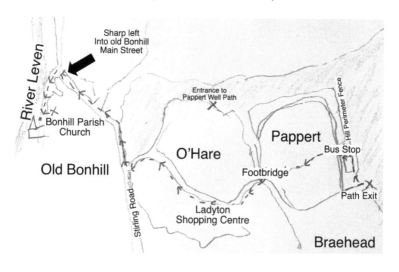

From the bus stop follow the path that skirts the playing pitch and go over the footbridge that crosses the main road (there are fantastic views of Glen Fruin from here) and walk down towards Ladyton Shopping Centre. Follow the road down until you reach Stirling Road again.

Follow it until there's a sharp left into Old Bonhill Main Street. With the chip shop on your right, you'll climb up the hill. Once you've passed the garage, take a sharp right into the grounds of Bonhill Parish Church.

The Housing Estates on the Hill and Old Bonhill

Bonhill was first mentioned in a charter in 1225. The Monks at Paisley Abbey were given fishing rights at Linbrane Pool on the River Leven and it was described as a Parish in 1270.

Its name had morphed from the original Buthehille to Bonhill by 1700. The parish had also enlarged by this time to include quite a bit of the Vale of Leven.

That drover's road we mentioned up at Pappert Well came all they way down the hill to a ford over the River Leven at Bonhill. From there it went on to Glasgow.

There was a church close by the river in 1747 but the one you can see today, the Bonhill Parish Church, was built in 1835.

The more recent estates you've walked through today, Pappert, O'Hare, Ladyton and Braehead are what is known as 'New Bonhill' and were said to have been built as 'overspill' housing for the people of Glasgow.

Up on the hill there are great views and an abundance of nature, as you've seen. But unemployment and hard times have meant certain parts have of the route have become a bit run down.

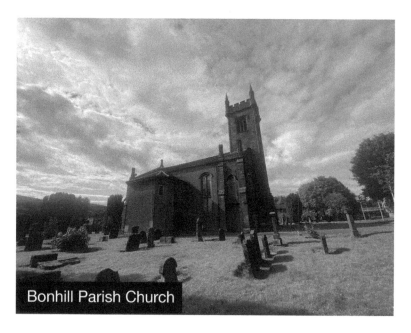

Bonhill Parish Church

Even where there is rubble and ruin nature will always prevail, and its appreciation can only be a good thing.

Hopefully, taking time to see some of the nice bits in this part of 'The Shire' has been worthwhile.

Walk Two

Bonhill Bridge - Balloch Station

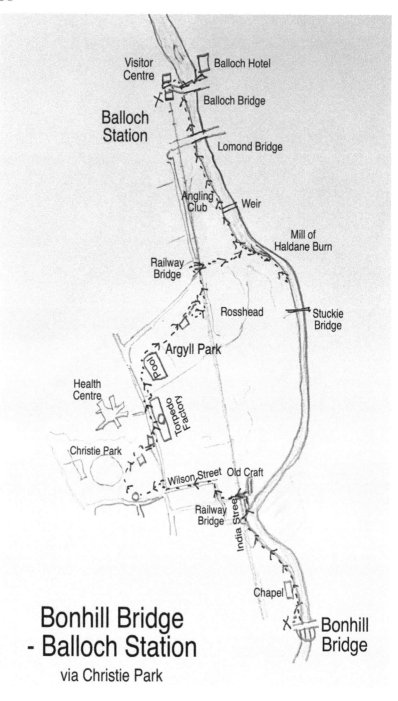

Visitor Centre

Balloch Hotel

Balloch Bridge

Balloch Station

Lomond Bridge

Angling Club

Weir

Mill of Haldane Burn

Railway Bridge

Rosshead

Stuckie Bridge

Argyll Park

Pool

Health Centre

Torpedo Factory

Christie Park

Wilson Street

Old Craft

Railway Bridge

India Street

Chapel

Bonhill Bridge
- Balloch Station
via Christie Park

Bonhill Bridge

Walk Two
Bonhill Bridge - Balloch Station

4km - Easy but two foot bridges to navigate

The start of the walk

(It's possible to miss out the first railway footbridge by going through the tunnel into Alexander Street and the second footbridge at Argyll Park by going along Lansbury Street instead. This will make the walk more accessible.)

Bonhill Bridge: The current bridge, known as The Rainbow Bridge, is only 2 mins walk from Alexandria Railway Station and was opened in July 1983.

Straight away you are stepping into nature. Feral pigeons inhabit the belly of the bridge, despite all efforts to put them off. Descendants of domestic pigeons who, in turn, came from cliff-dwelling Rock Doves, they have a strong presence in Alexandria. You'll find all colours of pigeon on this walk but look out for birds with two black bars on each light-grey wing. They look closer to their

Feral Pigeon

original ancestors. Pretty mixed up these days, genetically, you only find pure Rock Doves on remote north-western cliffs. These Bonhill pigeons often fall foul of Sparrow Hawks and Lesser Black-Backed Gulls. On

Lesser Black-backed Gull

the amber list of endangered species, worldwide, these aggressive gulls are very common in the Vale of Leven,

roosting and nesting here after feeding in nearby estuaries and refuse dumps.

Under Bonhill Bridge, there are some fantastic murals painted by local artist Barry the Cat. We'll see more of

Elements of the Old Bonhill Bridge

Barry's work soon.

Some elements of the previous bridge, known as The Whipple Bridge, have been reconstructed in the form of three pyramids on the north-western side of the new bridge. The Whipple Bridge dated back to 1898 and the four gas lamps that once stood on the four piers are on display here too. The original bridge on this site was instigated by Admiral Smollett in 1836 and was known as the Bawbee Bridge.

To my mind, the three mini Vale pyramids look a bit like the three Giza pyramids in Egypt which, in turn, were supposed to mirror Orion's Belt - formed by three bright stars called Alnitak, Alnilam and Mintaka.

It would also be remiss to leave out another great building that lies opposite the Bonhill Bridge. The four great pillars of Alexandria Public Hall give the building a very grand appearance.

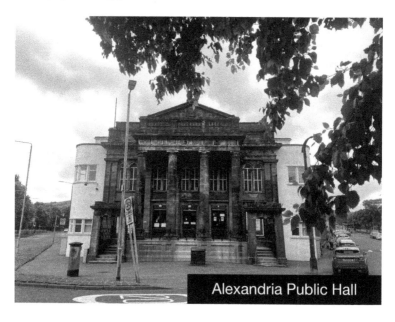
Alexandria Public Hall

Built in 1862 to house the Mechanics' Institute and its library, it was also used for functions and entertainment. Originally built to hold 800 people, it was soon extended to cope with 1100. Used as a library and a place where Mechanic's lectures could be given, live bands played there too. Some of the earliest moving pictures were shown there between 1899 and 1909. After that it was a music hall and theatre, eventually morphing into the Hall Cinema. This ran in competition with The Strand Cinema, situated further up Bank Street, until the early 70s.

The Rainbow bridge

Bonhill Bridge to India Street

Moving past the pyramids and the new, blue bicycle repair station we are soon on the River Leven cycle path heading towards Balloch. The river is said to be the second fastest river in Scotland after the Spey and is still popular with anglers. Salmon and Sea Trout are the fish of choice on this stretch. But a lot depends on the ebb and flow of the tides further down the river at Dumbarton as to whether these majestic creatures get this far. Some will head back to sea and some will race by on their way to Loch Lomond. Only a few will end up in the angler's net.

Before you get too far, you'll see some elderberry bushes on the left of the path. These are often coated in a black fungi that looks a bit like soot. It is known by quite a few different names including 'distillery fungus', 'distilleries' shadow', 'whisky fungus' and 'angels' share fungus'. *Baudoinia compniacensis* resides near distilleries and spirits maturation facilities. While it is not particularly nice

Long-tailed Tit

looking, it isn't harmful to people or animals. You can see it here in the picture above, but it didn't deter this Long-tailed Tit from spiralling through the branches in search of tiny spiders and caterpillars.

It's worth pausing at these murals and scanning the river

Female Goosander

which turns a big lazy corner at this point. You might see Goosanders here.

The female Goosander has a rust-coloured head with a crest and a serrated bill. They are fantastic fishers, diving down below the surface to hunt along the river bed. Displaying sexual dimorphism (the males and females look different), the male has a dark-green head with a red bill and has a white body with dark wings.

Kingfishers can be seen here from time to time too, racing over the surface - a blur of iridescent blue.

Stepping away from the river and through the little park behind the mural, you will see the small row of cottages that form India Street. The house nearest was called the 'Craft Hoose' and was said to have been for managers

India Street

and supervisors. You can still see the tall building at the end of the row. This was once part of The Craft or Alexandria Works.

India Street to Christie Park

Turn left at the end of India Street and up towards the green metal railway bridge. Going over, it's worth pausing a moment to look up North Street. With houses on the left and garages to the right, you can still see part of the Carman Hill above the town. In early summer the hill above the tree line is a mosaic of dark brown heather, bright green young ferns and a russet orange that marks last year's growth of bracken. I always get a real sense of where I am, and I was brought up here.

Walking past a small cottage on your right take a sharp right along Lennox Street to Wilson Street. Named after the man who first brought electricity to Dunbartonshire, Wilson Street leads up to Main Street and the gates of Christie Park. As an aside, Mr Wilson resided at Glenleven House for a while in Upper Smollett Street.

Christie Park used to be the site of the annual cattle show and was known as Notman's Park, then the School Park - before becoming Christie Park in 1902. Around 13 acres in all, it used to have a bandstand and a wooden pergola-type shelter.

WALK TWO

Tree Creeper

There's quite a bit of nature to be seen in the park. Apart from the Jackdaws and Magpies that peck away at the lawns you'll find Song Thrush, Blackbirds and even Tree Creepers.

These fascinating little birds are beautifully camouflaged against the bark of the sycamore and birch trees as they spiral up and along the trunks and branches. They probe for insects the nooks and crannies and will take shelter behind lose pieces of bark from the wind and rain. This one has managed to stuff about six insects into its beak all at once.

The Park takes its name it from John Christie who was one of the owners of The Craft. You just passed what remains of it, back in India Street.

It's said that he gifted the Park to the people of the Vale. But that's not how all his employees saw it at the time. In 1902, Christie, or perhaps somebody on the Craft board, decided that, instead of paying the employees an annual bonus, they would take the money and pay for a Park instead. For years after, it

The Cenotaph

was begrudgingly referred to as the 'Bonus Park'.

Christie Park was chosen for the site of the Vale Cenotaph. Unveiled on the 28th May 1921, it has over 360 names from Bonhill Parish who fell in the First World War, and more than 70, subsequently added, from World War Two.

Up near the gates that lead onto Middleton Street, you find the remains of the fountain. The lady once held a jug on her head. I still remember taking a

Lady minus water jug

long well-earned drink there after a day playing in the woods. The large patch of grass at the top of the park, before the woods, was once the putting green. There was a wee hut there too where you could buy crisps and little bottles of McDougall's Portello.

Christie Park to Vale Baths

Heading out of Christie Park, via the path next to the public toilets, you'll go back onto Main Street. A few steps northwards will take you to the old south lodge of Tulliechewan Castle. Built in 1792 and designed by the same architect who built Balloch Castle, Robert Lugar, the main part of Tulliechewan Castle was demolished using explosives in 1954.

On the opposite side of the street you can't miss what the locals call The Torpedo Factory. With its 540 foot long facade, impressive dome, giant pillars and Italian marble staircase, it was originally built as the Argyll Motor Factory for the equivalent of £27 million. The cars produced there were highly rated, with one model doing John O'Groats to Land's End in just 42 hrs and 5 mins.

After a few other incarnations the Royal Navy turned it into a torpedo factory in 1935 and it continued as such until 1969. It is said that a torpedo made there, a MK-8,

The Argyll Motor Works/Torpedo Factory

sank the General Belgrano during the Falklands War in May 1982. Now a home to shop outlets, you can go inside and have a look at that impressive marble staircase.

Moving on from the Torpedo Factory, north along the B857, you'll cross Heather Avenue to reach the gates of Argyll Park and, what is now, the path leading to the Vale of Leven Swimming Pool. Opened in 1973, the pool was a 'Godsend' to kids like myself who previously had to journey into the Brock Baths in Dumbarton.

The Vale Baths to the Stuckie Bridge

At first glance Argyll Park seems to be more of a sports centre - with its football pitches, tennis courts and bowling club, but there is plenty of wildlife to be found if you look.

A seemingly innocuous line of trees behind the bowling club often produces a few interesting sights. You might see Blackcaps, Goldfinches, Goldcrest and Siskins here as well as a whole host of insects - like the perfectly balanced Peacock Butterfly in the next picture.

Walking from these trees along the grassy border that edges the metal railway fence, **you often glimpse wild Rabbits and Starlings.** Continuing to the Lansbury

Peacock Butterfly

Street exit, you cross the metal railway bridge that takes you over the line into Rosshead. You actually end up in a little park with some nice grassy knolls. **In June these are covered in field forget-me-nots. There's even a small area of reeds where you'll find Yellow Iris.**

Continue on through the park and turn left towards Balloch rather than going over the footbridge to Jamestown.

You'll curve down and eventually reach the river. Walk back a little in the Bonhill direction and you'll see the Stuckie Bridge.

The Stuckie Bridge to Balloch Station

Once called the Stirling Bridge or the Drymen Bridge it was part of the railway network that ran east. It's now a pedestrian bridge that joins Rosshead to Jamestown. Built around 1877, it replaced an earlier wooden railway bridge. Interestingly, a Stuckie is the local word for a Starling.

Starling (Stuckie)

Before the railway came in 1850 the River Leven was used to transport goods down to the Clyde. At one time various works and factories lined the river. Huge chimney stacks belched smoke and man-made inlets diverted the river to power great machines. The first of these factories, the Dalquurn Works in Renton, was built in 1715. These factories employed more than 7000 workers at their peak. The last factory to close was the one we mentioned earlier - The Craft (an amalgamation of the Croftengea and Levenfield Works) in 1960.

Below the Stuckie Bridge, near the Mill of Haldane, there is a raised bank in the river. This is where you may be lucky enough to spot one of the river's most majestic creatures - the Mandarin Duck.

Mandarin Duck

This male bird has to be one of the most colourful creatures around. Originally from China they ended up in a whole host of gardens and parks in the 1800s. However, they began to escape and settle in the wild during the 1930s and are now regarded as a UK species.

Thought to be a sign of love and peace, you can see the males have a right go at each other at mating time. During these bouts the male flicks his head and displays that orange crest of his in a kind of over the top spat of fake preening. A species of wood duck, it can fly through dense woodland with ease. Although they're an 'alien' species, a bit like the Grey Squirrel, they don't seem to have caused any negative impact on the local flora or fauna.

I mentioned a raised pebble bank on the far side of the river, just to the right of an outlet channel that comes down through Jamestown from Haldane. It's worth

The Angling Club

having a closer look if you have binoculars. Apart from the Mandarin Duck, you might catch sight of Mallard Duck, Goosanders, Common Gull or even an Otter, if you're early enough.

If you're looking at that raised bank from the cycle path, behind you, in the woods, there is a series of old waterways, lades, that look a bit like the Everglades. If you're lucky and again, early enough, you might spot a Kingfisher in there. Moving on towards Balloch, you'll pass the Rowing Club on your left and after that the Vale of Leven District Angling Club. A two storey

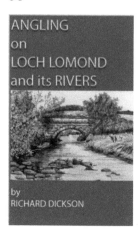

ANGLING
on
LOCH LOMOND
and its RIVERS

by
RICHARD DICKSON

wooden fronted building. The current clubhouse opened on the 20th of April 1974 and is run by anglers for anglers.

If you want to find out much more about fishing on the Leven and Loch Lomond I can thoroughly recommend a book called - *Angling on Loch Lomond and its Rivers* by local man, Richard Dixon.

Moving north passed the many moored boats and a few abandoned hulks, you eventually stand under the first of

The Lomond Bridge with Balloch Bridge behind

the two Balloch Bridges.

The Lomond Road Bridge, recently renovated and improved, was built in 1935. It was designed to connect the Dumbarton - Tarbert road to the main Dumbarton - Stirling road. Passing under this bridge you will see the final bridge of the nine now remaining over the River Leven - the Balloch Bridge. The first bridge here was built by Sir James Colquhoun of Luss in 1841. It lasted until 1887 when the second bridge was built. This one had one pedestrian path and a two-way road. Upgraded again in 2003/4, the current bridge has much better pedestrian access and meets the road standards now required.

Walking under this last bridge you will most-likely see the Sweeney boats that take passengers up the southern part of Loch Lomond.

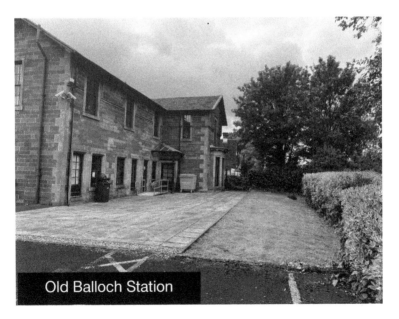

Old Balloch Station

Take a sharp left up the steep road that edges the bridge and you'll see the old Balloch Railway Station. Now a

WALK TWO

Visitor Centre. The view from the rear of the building shows the site of the original platform. The line ran another eight hundred metres from there to Balloch Pier.

Opposite the front of the Visitor Centre, you'll find your final destination - the current Balloch Railway Station.

The Current Balloch Station

By closing the Balloch Pier stop, it meant the level crossing that often held up the traffic on the main road could be removed. The new one-storey station was opened in April 1988 and is in the Loch Lomond and Trossach's National Park. From here you can go on to explore the Visitor Centre, Balloch Park, take a trip up the loch or dine in one of the many pubs and restaurants that line the main road.

However, if you want to add a final dash of nature to your walk, it's worth crossing Balloch Bridge and taking a sharp left, down by the Balloch Hotel.

Here, you can usually see Mallard Duck, Moorhen, Lesser Black-Backed Gulls, Black-Headed Gulls, and one of our largest water birds - the Mute Swan, pictured here with its cygnets. These 'ugly ducklings' will stay

Mute Swans

close to their parents over the summer months.

They'll remain an off-grey colour for about a year before changing into a white swan, but their bills won't take on the orange mantle until they are ready to breed.

Many people feed bread to the swans. I did it myself with my own kids once upon a time. But too much can cause them dietary problems. It's kinder to give them a piece of lettuce or veg…

The island in the middle of the Leven between Sweeney's boat yard and the Balloch Hotel is known locally as Monkey Island.

It's easy enough to walk back over the bridge to the new Balloch Railway Station and head home from there.

Walk Three

Bowling Harbour - Erskine Bridge

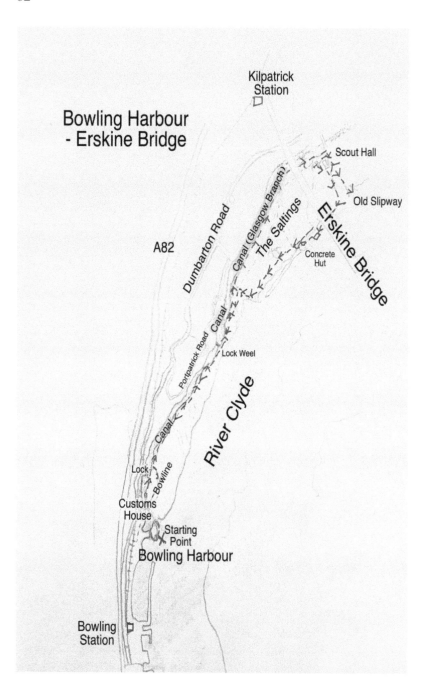

Kilpatrick
Station

Bowling Harbour
- Erskine Bridge

Scout Hall

Old Slipway

Dumbarton Road

Canal (Glasgow Branch)

The Saltings

Erskine Bridge

A82

Concrete
Hut

Portpatrick Road

Canal

Lock Weel

River Clyde

Canal

Lock

Bowline

Customs
House

Starting
Point

Bowling Harbour

Bowling
Station

Walk Three
Bowling Harbour - Erskine Bridge

4km - Easy - Flat, level surface all the way

Bowling Harbour to Erskine Bridge

You get to the arches of the old railway line at Bowling Harbour by car or perhaps by getting the train to Bowling Station and walking towards Glasgow along Dumbarton Road. A right turn once you pass under the railway bridge will take you down to Bowling Basin.

Once there, go under the old line and into the area dominated by the Customs House.

Walk right to the end of the path and look at the 'real harbour' with its skeletal scows and slime-covered stanchions.

Juvenile Cormorant

This is the real starting point of your walk. It's from this semi-circular railing overlooking the Clyde that you'll most likely see a Cormorant drying its wings.

This particular bird is a brown juvenile perched on some long-abandoned navigation marker. Red usually means 'keep left' or 'port' whereas green is normally 'starboard' or 'right'. But I'm only guessing here.

The Cormorant's wings are really too small for its body and are designed to get waterlogged. That way they can dive down deeper in search of fish. So, they need to drip-dry those feathers. You can usually tell which way the wind is coming from, as they'll swing round into it for maximum blow-dry effect.

Walking back past a big red boat called the Seahorse, which used to be a research boat and trawler, you can take a better look at the slightly shabby beach on your right.

Pied Wagtail

There is life down there and if see a flash of black and white, it's most likely going to be a Wagtail. Constantly flicking its tail, this handsome bird bobs up and down, fluttering up to catch insects on the wing.

We have three common wagtail species in West Dunbartonshire - the Grey Wagtail, which is actually white and grey with a yellow rump, the White Wagtail and the Pied Wagtail.

The Pied is actually considered to be a subspecies of the White and is usually more sooty under the wing or on the flank in the summer as it still hasn't finished its moult.

The Wagtail has a fairly harsh chirp which brings me to a point. More often than not, you'll hear a bird before you see it, especially if your eyesight is rubbish like mine.

Goldfinch

The Goldfinch is another bird you might hear then see on the beach. It produces a long burst of song full of trills and chirps that is bright and uplifting.

This Goldfinch, on Bowling Beach, is feeding on a species saltwater succulent. You'll normally find them in large groups feeding on seed heads.

There seems to be more Goldfinches these days. Compared to the 1990s, there's reported to be as many as eight times the number now. On the other hand, Greenfinch numbers have taken a tumble. 59% down in the last ten years. It's thought that a parasite-induced bacterial infection may be the cause there.

Bowling Harbour has been an important site for literally thousands of years.

The Romans built a fort and bathhouse here to mark the western most point of the Antonine Wall. A final frontier in 144AD. And in more recent times, it marked the western end of the Forth and Clyde Canal.

This lock system allows boats to take a massive shortcut along Scotland's narrowest stretch - from Bowling to Grangemouth.

Two railway lines ran through here at one time. And you can still see the swing bridge to the right of the Customs House that the let ships with high masts pass through.

The black and white Customs House, built in the early 19th century, has just been refurbished and the archways under the tracks now house cafes and shops.

Walk back towards the swing bridge and under the arch you first came through, and you'll soon arrive at an

Bowling Customs House

impressive lock system that takes you up to the Forth and Clyde Canal towards Glasgow.

Designed by John Smeaton, work on the canal began in 1768, but it didn't opened until 1790 due to money problems.

Once bustling with merchant ships, scows, barges and fishing boats, all vying for their turn to go through the lock systems, the canal is much quieter and, I suppose, cleaner now.

You can actually walk or cycle the whole 35 miles to Grangemouth on the path you're on now.

As you toddle past the lock systems and flank the canal proper, you may find Mute Swans nesting by the path. They sometimes put some red fencing around the nests to stop dogs getting at the birds and the birds getting at you.

Mute Swan Nest

Apart from a loud warning hiss, swans have been known to give people a good whack with their wings. The male, known as a cob, may become quite aggressive if you invade their space. So, give them a wide berth.

Walking along the canal path towards Glasgow, you'll find a wide variety of plants and flowers in the summer. And it's amongst this wild backdrop that you'll discover just as much drama and excitement as any African savannah.

Herbivores try to harvest as much as they can from the grasses, flowers and plants while predators patrol the skies and waterways in search of a decent protein snack. Some, of course, like spiders, lie in wait. When it comes to insects, basically everything eats everything. This Meadow Plant Bug, spotted a few yards along the path is well camouflaged and might be considered a solitary herbivore.

WALK THREE

Meadow Plant Bug

A pest of any grass crop it will cause the seed heads to shrivel. A relative of the Bed Bug and the Aphid, the Meadow Plant Bug has a long straw-like tube called a rostrum that it forces into the plant to extract nutrients.

It can fly between plants, but if it does it risks being spotted by the next, rather dazzling creature you may encounter by the cycle track.

A few feet away, perched on a Butterbur leaf, a Common Darter could be waiting patiently for its next meal. This relatively small species of dragonfly is an ambush predator that uses a favoured vantage point to survey the canal path.

It waits until it sees what it wants passing by and then gives chase. Harmless to humans, it's unlikely to be you.

Common Darter

I think this may be a mature male as its abdomen has a red hue. Young males and females are yellow or brown. Also, its pterostigma - (those dots at the front of its wings) are a browny-red colour. Females can have quite a selection of wing-dot colours, including blue.

The Butterbur leaf, this Darter's favourite spot, is similar in shape and size to rhubarb. Unbelievably, it gets its name because people used the big leaves to wrap and preserve butter.

These ancient plants are plentiful in the summer on the canal path. So, if you're ever caught in a summer monsoon, *like what I was one day*, they make pretty decent umbrellas.

Walking further along the canal towards Glasgow, you will see some house boats on the opposite bank. After

Moorhen with chick

WALK THREE

these, you may spy a Kingfisher, if you're lucky, on some of the lower branches. This part of the canal is called the Glasgow Branch and you will pass some houses, again on the opposite side, whose gardens extend down to the waterside. It's around here that you should be able to catch a glimpse of a Moorhen.

The one in the previous picture is feeding a young chick some vegetation. Moorhens are often confused with Coots but the difference is in the bill colour. Moorhen's are bright red whereas Coots have a white bill and mantle. The coot is also a little bigger and will dive out of sight rather than skulk away.

A few hundred yards further on and you'll reach a small lock/bridge that takes you over the canal to Portpatrick Road. Don't cross over. Keep on the canal path and continue all the way to the Erskine Bridge.

The Erskine Bridge

The Erskine Bridge, one of the most iconic landmarks in West Dumbartonshire, is technically in Renfrewshire too. 145 feet above your head, if you look up and listen, you can hear the traffic bumping over some of the 15 spans that join the bridge together.

Opened on the 2nd of July, 1972, it's a mile long and was built to give enough clearance for most of the shipping traffic below. In 1996, however, an oil rig called the Texaco Captain collided with the road deck and caused the bridge to be closed for some time.

It cost over £10 million to build the bridge but it recouped over £30 million in 60p tolls between 1972 and 2006. That's when the Scottish Government scrapped all tolls in Scotland.

WALK THREE

Old Ferry Slipway

Erskine Bridge back to Bowling Harbour

Of course, before the bridge existed, ferries took the traffic across the river Clyde and, if you go under the bridge and continue until you get to the Erskine Ferry Road, you'll be able to walk down and see what's left of the slipways.

You have just skirted a local nature reserve known as The Saltings so it's worth coming back up the road, past the Scout Hall again, and then turning into the reserve.

Once boggy farmland, the area was filled with rubble in the 60s during the bridge's construction. This initially killed off most of the plant and animal life but it also dried out the area allowing a different ecology to evolve.

The Magpie Moth

As I said in my introduction, life has a way of 'finding a way', and now the area is teaming with it.

If it's the right day for it, normally in mid-July, you might come across a little snow storm of Magpie Moths. Like confetti, they flutter clumsily through the bushes and alight on just about anything.

There seems to be a lot of wild raspberries scattered around the area, which may be one of the reasons the moths are here. Easy to misidentify as a butterfly, its distinctive wing patterns warn off predators, hinting at a very nasty taste if they bite.

WALK THREE

Before you explore the big flat area known as The Saltings it's worth cutting down on to the path through the woods on the Glasgow side of the Erskine Bridge.

Then curve round, past a tangle of Meadow Sweet and Wild Raspberries until you pass under the bridge and onto the lonely shore below.

Stepping down onto this slightly shabby beach in the shadow of bridge above, you'll find the remains of a concrete hut. It's as if it has fallen off something that no longer exists.

Graffiti strewn, it lies at an angle at the edge of the water, to me, a sad reminder of the many poor souls that

Concrete Hut

have taken their lives by jumping from the bridge above.

At one point up to 36 people a year took the 125 plunge. Very few survived.

Thankfully, they have now installed a high barrier along the bridge footpath, which may deter a few.

That lonely hut makes me think about one of the reasons I've written this wee book. People speak about mindfulness, well-being and mental health. Can nature help us focus, put things into perspective? I'm not sure. All I know is that it that, for me, it is a beautiful distraction that still fills me with a child-like sense of wonder. That little wave of exhilaration, that rush of endorphins actually makes me smile and feel more positive.

There's a strip of land here pinched between the Clyde and a smaller tributary known as the Dalnottar Burn.

Curlew

It's here that you might spot Curlews, poking around in the mud. A saltwater estuary, the Clyde still has seaweed and even crabs as this point. You're much more likely to see Curlews nearer Dumbarton but it's worth a look.

With a wingspan of almost a metre the Curlew is our largest wading birds. Its curved bill, at 15cm or so, is an amazing adaptation that lets it probe right down into the wet sand or seaweed and accurately locate its prey.

The tip of their bills are extremely sensitive and it can distinguish prey from non prey. There is also a good chance that they can hear what they're after, as the initial stab of the beak seems far from random. Once it gets its prey it then has to flick it all the way back up that slender bill into its mouth.

Oystercatcher

You may also spot Oystercatchers on this same stretch. A bird you'll often hear peeping above your head as it flies about trying to find the best spot to land. Its long red bill and black and white plumage are a giveaway. If you climb up the beach a little and look down into the Dalnottar Burn, you may also see Mallard Duck and Heron amongst the mud and the reeds.

Walking back up from the Clyde to the path on the lower part of the Saltings, there are some tall reed beds and hogweed down by the Dalnottar Burn. It's here that you can find another summer migrant - The Sedge Warbler.

Often seen clinging onto a reed or perched on some swinging flower-head, singing its heart out, this little bird has a characteristic black and white eye stripe.

The Sedge Warbler is another bird I don't remember from my youth. There are now more than quarter of a

Sedge Warbler

million pairs in the UK but there is concern that their winter habitat may shrink as parts of Africa get drier.

They have a very orange gape when they sing and the males, in particular, will repeat phrases.

It's worth retracing your steps a little by going back up and under the bridge again to the entrance of the Saltings. Walking through this archway will take you through some woodland full of wild flowers.

You should see Red Campion Flowers jutting up from the forest floor and Great Tits in the canopy above. Blue Tits and Willow Warblers will be searching the bushes for insects too, but there's one bird in particular you should definitely hear. This bird's complicated trill

Wren

will pierce the forest and cut through any rumbling traffic noise from that bridge above.

The Wren has one of the loudest songs you'll encounter in the area. They sing over twenty notes per second and at a volume ten times that of a crowing rooster, by equivalent weight. They have a special chamber called a syrinx which helps amplify their call to an impressive 90 decibels.

When you hear this incredible blast of song, it only seems to be a few feet away. And it probably is. But you try and find the culprit. The Wren is so tiny and well camouflaged that you might even wander off, simply giving up. Look for a potential vantage point between a metre and three metres above the ground.

They have a delicate dome-shaped nest with an entrance hole. It's usually made of feathers, moss, lichen and leaves. The female will often lay more than ten eggs at a time. This is our second smallest bird next to the

Goldcrest

Goldcrest. Another bird you can see here, perhaps picking green caterpillars from a Willow tree.

Not too obvious in this Goldcrest picture, captured by pure luck, it has a Mohican-type blast of yellow on top of its tiny head. The Wren is still our shortest bird but the Goldcrest is a few grams lighter, at around 5.5g.

Walking on and back out into the sunshine, or possibly the rain, you'll see the Saltings proper - a wide expanse of meadow with a proliferation of grasses and wildflowers.

Once a boggy marsh, this area is now full of flowers like the blue Meadow Crane's Bill. There are snowy clouds

WALK THREE

of Meadow Sweet, rafts of Hogweed and, of course, the soil enhancing Red Clover.

Red Clover

Red Clover tends to fix more nitrogen than White Clover in its first two years. But what is 'nitrogen fixing'? Clover has nodules on its roots that contain bacteria. These bacteria convert nitrogen in the air to nitrates in the soil. These nitrates, in turn, are important for foliage development. So any plants in the same location will benefit.

Following the path beside the Dalnottar Burn, head back towards the Clyde and the metal swan sculptures just before the shore.

Down by the burn, more often than not, beneath a wet stone, you can find a pretty wonderful, little amphibian. Dark brown or sometimes slightly orange in colour, the Common Newt is an amazing creature.

Common Newt

If you do find one, you're looking at one of the most successful creatures on the planet. Amphibians like this wee guy have been here, uninterrupted, for over 370 million years. They've lasted twice as long as the dinosaurs and 180 times longer than us. As larvae in water they breathe through external gills and prey on tadpoles and other small creatures.

Once they move to the land, they breathe through their skin but also have lungs. They don't have a rib cage that expands and contracts so instead they take air into their bodies by moving the chin-skin underneath their head. They can mate after about three years and generally live for six. This one eventually crawled under my camera for shelter.

Continue on past the metal swans, until the path bears right. Then you'll come to a crossroads of sorts. Turn left and go through the trees, keeping a few glimpses of the Clyde on your left. Eventually, you'll pass some old railway buildings and end up back on the canal path. You'll recognise the wheel mechanism at the lock where you can cross to Portpatrick Road.

Wheel at Lock

Continue back along the path towards Bowling, enjoying the wild flowers and the canal.

There is a new piece of walkway you can cut down on to called the Bowline. Opened in partnership with Scottish

Canals in 2021, this 'active travel bridge' reuses the old railway and has been imaginatively lined with historic pictorial facts about the canal and rail system in the area. This information takes the form of giant posters in a timeline along the old railway bridge.

You can either continue along this new, very accessible route to Bowling Station or return to your car if you have one parked.

Just a wee word of warning about parking your car right down in the cobbled area dominated by the Harbour Customs House. This is an area that is locked at certain times.

Gates don't open until 8.15am so, if you don't get back to your car before they lock up at 17.45pm, it could be a long night…

Walk Four

Goldenhill Park - The Cochno Stone

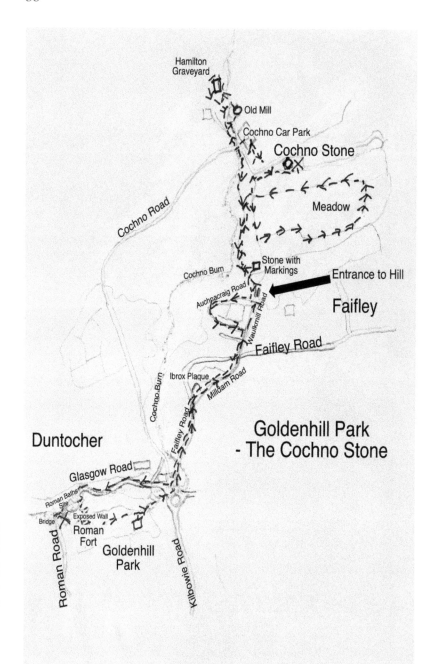

Hamilton
Graveyard

Old Mill

Cochno Car Park

Cochno Stone

Cochno Road

Meadow

Cochno Burn

Stone with
Markings

Entrance to Hill

Auchpacraig Road

Naulknill Road

Faifley

Faifley Road

Ibrox Plaque

Milldam Road

Cochno Burn

Faifley Road

Duntocher

Goldenhill Park
- The Cochno Stone

Glasgow Road

Roman Baths
Site

Exposed Wall

Bridge

Roman
Fort

Goldenhill
Park

Roman Road

Kilbowie Road

WALK FOUR

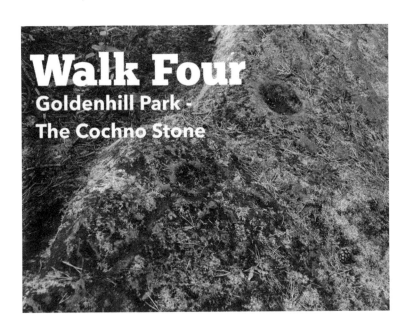

Walk Four
Goldenhill Park - The Cochno Stone

6km - Medium - Steep sections and the odd rough path

Goldenhill Park to Waulking Mill Road

This walk will take you back some 5000 years in time, as well as introducing you to some of the stunning nature on the hills above Duntocher and Faifley..

You can park in the car park, just off Roman Road, next to the Duntocher Burn. But there are buses to Glasgow Road in Duntocher and the nearest railway station is probably Singer Station.

It's worth taking a look over the bridge on Roman Road, at the Duntocher Burn before you enter Goldenhill Park where the war memorial stands.

The Dipper

Known as the Roman Bridge, there may well have been a Roman crossing there at one time but the current structure was actually constructed in the Eighteenth Century and rebuilt after bomb damage in 1943.

This dark, meandering section of water is ideal for a bird called the Dipper. An amazing wee bird that does what it says on the tin. This aquatic songbird bobs up and down about 60 times every minute. On the up in numbers, this little underwater hunter is looking for things like Caddis Fly larvae and Minnows on the river bed.

They can walk underwater and will happily overturn stones and rummage about until their find their prey. Well-adapted for river foraging, they have natural goggles, highly oxygenated blood and even flaps that cover their nostrils.

Site of Roman Bath-house

Leaving the bridge enter the gates of Goldenhill Park and stand next to the war memorial.

You are now standing on the spot where the Romans had a Bathhouse in 148AD. Close your eyes and imagine... Roman soldiers standing in the steam room, covered in oil. Then imagine them scraping the oil, dirt and dead skin from their bodies with a curved hook-like implement known as a strigil.

Roman soldiers often frequented the baths after their eight hour shift at about two in the afternoon. You might have heard the panting of the weightlifters, the pummelling of the masseuses, singing echoing up from the baths or even the screams coming from the section given over to the armpit plucker.

Wandering between the cold room, the tepid room and the hot room, they wore special sandals called sculponea. These had thick, wooden soles to protect their feet from the scalding floor tiles. Excavated in the

1780s by Glasgow University, they found a female statuette at the site. This is now in the Huntarian Museum.

After your little dunk in the baths, stroll up the hill towards a fenced off area on the slope. If you peer through the bars here, you'll see an exposed part of the actual Antonine Wall.

A Section of the Antonine Wall

What you're looking at is a small section of the wall rampart stone foundation. The word Duntocher means 'the fort on the causeway'. If you want a better look at this railed off section and the fort on the hill above, go to the Clydesider YouTube channel. There is a nice one-minute video with some aerial shots of both.

Goldenhill Park is a place where you really have to use your imagination to get any semblance of the Romans and their presence there. You may be able to read some of the vandalised notice boards if you're lucky, but if not, a rough description of the wall would be as follows…

Built on the orders of Emperor Antoninus Pius, the wall spanned a 40 mile stretch all the way from Bowling to Boness in the east. It marked the final frontier of the Roman Empire in 144 AD.

Mainly constructed by laying turf on a stone base, like the section of the foundation exposed behind the railings, it would have been flanked by a 12m wide ditch. Some 3m deep, it would have helped keep the

A Wooden Roman Centurion

marauding Caledonians at bay.

The Romans didn't linger long in Duntocher. It was only about twenty years before they retreated south to the relative safety of Hadrian's Wall.

In Goldenhill, the Council usually mark out the position of the Roman Fort on the crest of the hill by cutting the grass where the walls would have been. You'll find these markings north of the trig point.

What *is* evident in Goldenhill Park is an abundance of wild flowers - Meadow Buttercups, Hogweed, Ground Elder, Meadow Crane's-bill and Forget-Me-Nots pepper the grassy hillsides.

Follow the path up to the two wooden Roman soldiers at the school playground then wind your way down to the exit at the roundabout.

Metal Arch and small brick plaque

Continue over the roundabout, following Faifley Road, up the hill until you reach the new metal arch and the small commemoration plaque in memory of the three Faifley men who died during the Ibrox Disaster on the 2nd of January 1971.

I would have been at this match myself, had my cousin not partaken of too much drink the night before.

There was a crush in the crowd during the 'Old Firm Match' that day which resulted in 66 dead and over 200 injured. An awful event that has haunted Rangers vs Celtic matches over the years.

Taking a right from Faifley Road, you can cut up Milldam Road, past the mini market, onto Faifley Road again, where you take a right, past the church, and then a left up Waulking Mill Road. This will take you to the

Entrance onto the hill

entrance to the path that goes onto the hill above Faifley.

Entrance to Path to The Cochno Stone

As soon as you walk onto the hill, you might hear a Chiffchaf or a Willow Warbler. Two very similar looking birds, it's their very different calls that really tell them apart. The Chiffchaff, named after its call, has a repetitive, harsh *chiff - chaff* whereas the Willow Warbler has a descending musical song that sounds, to me, like a

WALK FOUR

leaf sailing down to earth - every note lower than the

Willow Warbler

one before.

Follow the path and keep left until you're walking beside a stream. This is the Cochno Burn. There are various

Cochno Burn

little cuttings that take you to the water's edge and even a grassy patch that is quite open. It's here that you should find quite a selection of butterflies and diurnal moths. All a bit weather dependant, of course.

I had to walk into quite a thick patch of nettles, but it was worth it to catch a glimpse of the Chimney Sweep Moth. Smaller than a Ringlet Butterfly and black rather than dark brown, it still has a thin white edge to its upper wings.

The Chimney Sweep Moth

There were quite a few dog walkers with packs that splashed around in the stream but that's cool. The hill should be for everyone. Not just some guy with a camera who's chasing moths through the undergrowth.

Eventually you wind up the stream and bear right until you reach a crossroads in the path. One route heads down to the right. Another continues to follow the stream up to the Cochno car park. I chose to go right and across, away from the stream and into the woods.

This path cuts along the side of the hill until there is another less distinct path heading up and left, through a stunning meadow.

You'll ultimately cut through the meadow to the higher parallel path going back the way you came. However, it's worth lingering in the meadow. It's summer and the wild flowers are at their best. Take a moment to stand still and take in the scent. A bit like this member of the Order Lepidoptera, below.

The Latticed Heath Moth

The Latticed Heath Moth is another diurnal (daytime) moth. Similar in size to the Chimney Sweep, it likes slightly more open countryside. Seen over the summer, its larva feed on clover and trefoils until things get a little colder. When the days get shorter, it spins a cocoon within which the caterpillar produces a hard, sub-dermal skin. The outer skin moults away and the hard skin toughens even more to form a pupa. Perfect for staying snug and protected over the winter months.

Once through the meadow, you'll find a more substantial path heading left again. This will eventually lead you to the site of the Cochno Stone. But there are still a few things to see along the way. In the darker sections of the wooded path that will take you back to the Cochno Burn, you'll notice something moving along the trunks and branches. Once only found in England, the Nuthatch is a stunning wee tree weaver that is becoming more and more common in West Dunbartonshire. First spotted in Scotland in the 1980s, this bird has successfully integrated into our woodland communities.

You'll see it flicking the moss away to reveal the bugs below but it will also eat fruit and nuts. Unlike the Tree creeper, which tends to face up the tree, the Nuthatch is

Nuthatch

just as happy pointing down the way. It often has caches of food stored behind lose pieces of bark that will keep it going for up to thirty days.

Pic1

Heading up through the dark wood, with the Cochno Burn on your left you will arrive at the Cochno Car Park. From here head back towards the top parallel path, but take a cut through the ferns, heading up the hill again towards a dry stone dyke with some rusty

Pic 2

metal rails on top. Follow this wall back in the direction of the car park again. This is where every bit of your

WALK FOUR

Sherlock Holmes ingenuity will be required. If you're lucky, you'll reach a raised mound, marked as a red diamond in Pic 1.

Pic 2 was taken from the yellow X in Pic 1. The same tree is circled in yellow and the nearest yellow line, marks the stone dyke that should be on your right. The stone dyke, marked in yellow straight lines, cuts in to form a V around the most easterly part of the stone.

The green wavy line highlights a few evergreen conifers on the northern edge of the buried stone. Are you with me so far?

You might spot a piece of exposed stone at the base of the Cochno red diamond. I've marked this with a blue circle in Pic 1 and Pic 4.

Pic 3

But all the really important stuff - the Bronze Age carvings, the cup and ring marks…even a pair of feet, each with four toes rather than the customary five, were all buried under several feet of earth in 1968. Handy!

Although this was done for their own protection, it's still, in my opinion, a total waste and a complete anti-climax. There was a more recent unearthing in 2016 by Glasgow University where they recorded their findings in much more detail. That particular excavation is detailed on a YouTube video https://youtu.be/s1LqWH0IqIs

Pic 4

It would be much better to let people see what's under there in some kind of controlled manner. This 13m x 8m, diamond-shaped stone (marked in red in Pic 1), now buried under the grass and ferns, is one of Northern Europe's most significant Prehistoric sites! 'Open this up. Construct a glass walkway over it. Make it a feature of the area rather than a dirty secret!' would be my cry.

Pic 3 shows three figures standing in a rough diamond shape. This is the Cochno Stone. Marked in red in Pic 1.

Cochno Stone back to Goldenhill Park

However, all is not lost. There is still a way to see some of those 5000-year markings, but you should make a small detour first. So, get yourself back to the Cochno Car Park and go out of the main entrance, heading into the woods on the road that leads to the Glasgow Vet School Farm. After only a few yards, go over a mound on your right and wind down to the Cochno Burn again.

Here, you should find the remains of an old mill, or at least the stone foundations of an old mill wheel and a sluice gate further up the burn.

Old Cochno Burn Mill

You should still be able to see where the wheel sat in the burn and where the mechanism was housed.

Most of the industry in Faifley came from water power. The Cochno Burn was so important. There was a dye works and eventually four cotton mills employing over 1400 people. However, The American Civil War in 1861 put a stop to the trade and forced three of the mills to close. I'll let you think about the whole morality of that hidden history for a moment before we move on.

Continue up the hill, following the burn until you climb quite a steep hill. It's at the top of this hill that you'll find another, more recent link to the past.

The Hamilton family graveyard is situated in the woods here.

Hamilton Family Graveyard

With most of the railing rotted away or removed, there are still a few family members buried there. The lands around Cochno were transferred from the ownership of the Paisley Abbey monks to the Hamilton family before the Reformation. Andrew Hamilton obtained Cochno in 1550 but lost it soon after after picking the wrong side in the Battle of Langside. The Crown restored the estates 24 years later and it remained in the family until 1900. The grave stones on this site include one dedicated to Claud Hamilton Hamilton, his first wife, Henrietta Anne Bruce, and his second wife Nora. Claud's full title was Claud Hamilton Hamilton of Barns, Cochna and Dunmore. He died at the age of 77 but it's said that his body is actually in Dunmore Park, near Stirling.

I mentioned that there was still a way of seeing, first hand, some of those 5000-year-old Bronze Age carvings... So...

If you go back to the Cochno Car Park and follow the Cochno burn down, almost as far as the entrance to the hill on Waulkmill Road.

By the way, a waulkmill at Cochno was mentioned in charters going back as far as 1643. A waulkmill being a place where people finished cloth, often using Fuller's Earth (an absorbent clay material) to bind the fibres tighter.

Big Stone in the Glade

WALK FOUR

Just before you get to the entrance to the hill, you'll see a path to your left. Go up that path for about fifty yards until you see a cleared area on your left. Walk into the small glade and **you'll see a big stone surrounded by some baby rhododendrons and mountain ash. Now take a closer look at the stone surface.**

Looking carefully, you will see several Bronze Age cup marks along with, what looks like a figure with some kind of circle enclosing its head.

Figure with cup mark above

There is great conjecture over the origins and meanings of these markings.

Some say that the circles represent the orbits of various planets and that they show links to an ancient sun god who had a battle with an evil serpent. But, I'm guessing we will never know what the ancient people of these hills were really trying to convey.

Needless to say, we are fortunate to have such an artistic and mystical link to our past on our doorstep.

After pondering our ancestors and their beliefs for a moment, make for the entrance to Waulking Mill Road but instead of going through the same gate you came in, stay on the hill and take the exit onto Auchnacraig Road.

This proved worthwhile on my last summer walk here as I saw a few more butterflies - a Red Admiral dancing around some nettles and a Meadow Brown, landing on the path in front of me. Teasing me to get closer, only to fly away again when I almost got it in focus.

Meadow Brown

It eventually landed on some Creeping Thistle flower heads and posed like a true pro, its proboscis prodding for nectar.

The Meadow Brown is in what I call the 'dithery group of butterflies'. These are the ones that never quite know where or if they are ever going to land.

Meadow Browns can occur in pretty big groups and will often fly in dull weather when many other species are lying low. The males tend to be more active, patrolling their vantage points. The females are often found resting further down in the grass. They lay their eggs by aerial dispersal in the first four days of their very short 5-12 day lifespan.

The best sighting, however, was of three young Bullfinches gathering seeds and flying about in the bushes. Mainly brown, they still hadn't developed their black cap or, for that matter, totally come clean as to whether they were male (pink chest) or female (brown chest). Take the path to Faifley Road and retrace your route, turning into Glasgow Road at the roundabout as you go back to the start.

Young Bullfinch

I hope you've enjoyed these four summer strolls through West Dunbartonshire and its wonders.

Meanwhile - explore, pause, think, wonder and enjoy every morsel of life you can. Each second is precious. Each new discovery - a minor miracle.

Some Summer Flowers of West Dunbartonshire

(Top left to bottom right)
Large Yellow Loosestrife, The Creeping Thistle, Bull Thistle, Velezia, Autumn Hawkbit

Harebell, Fireweed (Willowherb), Hairy Willowherb, Himalayan Balsam, Devil's-bit

Knapweed, Bramble, Yarrow, Fuchsia, Bog Asphodel

Corn Rocket (Southern Warty Cabbage), Chamomile, Broom, Foxglove, Meadow Buttercup

Bindweed, Red Clover, Large Yellow Loosefire, Marsh Thistle, Heath Spotted Orchid

Meadow Crane's-bill, Sticky Willy, Cross-leaved Heath,
Fox and Cubs, American Speedwell

Greater Stitchwart, Wild Angelica, Red-Stalk Aster, Bittersweet Nightshade, Holy Rope

WALK FOUR

Paul Murdoch is a full-time writer, presenter, photographer and musician who has eight novels in publication. Over the last ten years, he's been fortunate enough to work in schools and libraries all over the UK, Malaysia and Europe. He's visited over 40,000 children in that time, giving interactive workshops and presentations. Paul presents on nature and well-being and has penned two slightly tongue-in-cheek fitness books - *Old Bloke Goes Running* and *Old Bloke Goes Swimming*.

www.paulmurdoch.co.uk

Other Books in this Series